JAMES HANSEN

WINNING THE WAR WITH PTSD

The Workbook for *KISSING THE TARMAC*

WINNING THE WAR WITH PTSD

The Workbook for *KISSING THE TARMAC*

Winning the War With PTSD: The Workbook for Kissing the Tarmac

Copyright © 2016 by James Hansen

ISBN 978-0-692-79157-8

All rights reserved. No part of this book may be reproduced or transmitted in any form or by any means, electronic or mechanical, including photocopying, without the express written consent of the author, except where permitted by law.

Cover photo courtesy of *Washington Post*

Book design by Stories To Tell, www.StoriesToTellBooks.com

Contents

Author Biography	vii
Introduction	ix
How the Instructor Can Use This Workbook	xi
A Summary of *Kissing the Tarmac*	xv
Section 1	1
Lesson 1	5
Lesson 2	7
Lesson 3	9
Lesson 4	11
Lesson 5	13
Lesson 6	15
Lesson 7	17
Lesson 8	19
Lesson 9	21
Lesson 10	23
Lesson 11	25
Section 2	27
Lesson 12	29
Lesson 13	31
Lesson 14	33
Lesson 15	35
Lesson 16	37
Lesson 17	39
Lesson 18	41

Lesson 19	43
Lesson 20	45
Lesson 21	47
Lesson 22	49
Lesson 23	51
Resources	53
Acknowledgements	55

Author Biography

James Hansen based his memoir on actual combat experiences while serving in the Vietnam War with Charlie Company, 2/501st Infantry, 101st Airborne Division in 1968-69. He spent over four decades recovering from Post Traumatic Stress Disorder (PTSD). Mr. Hansen didn't seek counseling until 2006. It was during this time his therapist recommended he write out his war experiences. The author found the exercise to be so beneficial he continued writing and began his memoir in 2008, a process that lasted eight years.

Mr. Hansen earned a BA in urban and regional planning from Eastern Washington State University in 1971 and completed the University of Denver's Executive Management Program in 1978. Following a thirty–eight year public sector career in the fields of city planning, management and economic development, he opened a private consulting practice in Long Beach, California in 2008.

From 2012 to 2014, Mr. Hansen served as executive director of U.S. VETS-Long Beach, a nationwide nonprofit providing critical services and shelter to 550 homeless veterans each day. He was responsible for several programs including those assisting veterans with Traumatic Brain Injury (TBI) and PTSD. Currently, he is a business advisor with the Goldman Sachs 10,000 Small Businesses Program at Long Beach City College.

Mr. Hansen resides in Southern California with his wife Pamela.

INTRODUCTION

Winning the War With PTSD is a workbook companion to *Kissing The Tarmac*, a Vietnam War memoir focused on the development and resolution of symptoms associated with PTSD.

While the memoir offers inspiration and hope to those experiencing PTSD, no matter the cause, this workbook provides specific learning objectives to gain more understanding of both symptom development and resolution techniques.

This is a *layman's* approach to the topic, unlike most PTSD-related publications written by professionals in the mental health field. Many veterans can relate to the author's military experience and find his recommendations applicable. This workbook complements the fine publications and practices of the Veterans Administration, nonprofit organizations like U.S. VETS, independent professional counselors and researchers.

The memoir and this workbook can be utilized most effectively in group therapy sessions where the Learning Objectives can be experienced in depth by individuals challenged by PTSD.

The subject matter of *Winning the War With PTSD* is timely. An estimated twenty percent of the 3,000,000 veterans returning from the wars in Iraq and Afghanistan since 2004 suffer from PTSD. About thirty percent of Vietnam War veterans still struggle with the symptoms. Civilians also develop PTSD from a range of traumatic experiences on an ongoing basis.

The theme of the book is how a young man subjected to a sustained period of acute stress from combat develops PTSD during and following the war. Decades later the symptoms strengthen affecting his life at several levels. He eventually finds an effective path to healing and redemption after years of struggle. His success has application to all combat veterans and civilians alike facing similar PTSD-related challenges.

As for the style of the book, there is a strong quality of self-awareness and reflection so the reader sees his rational and emotional states equally.

A unique feature that distinguishes *Kissing The Tarmac* from other books written by combat veterans about PTSD is employed. Each chapter describing his war experience begins with a passage from his daily journal and ends with a subject-related letter home. The narrative is positioned between the two.

This structure offers a *compare and contrast* opportunity for the reader to observe how patterns of behavior develop when James reacts to traumatic situations.

The approach creates a window into his thought process. Horrific events are revealed that he tried to put behind him. The reader comes to understand why the road to his recovery, like so many others with PTSD, was long and difficult.

How the Instructor Can Use This Workbook

READING, SPEAKING, AND WRITING

Educators have long known there is a powerful relationship between reading, speaking, and writing. In particular, reading another person's true story engages a learner in a social, peer-to-peer relationship with the author. In this program, reading allows the class participant to understand the mind and heart of another PTSD sufferer even more so than through face-to-face interaction.

Yet a reader must do more than just read a book to gain the deeper benefits that these lessons offer. On the simplest level, the act of speaking about a book one has read will always have a powerful benefit: the reader must construct and communicate their own point of view toward what they have read.

The most basic and least challenging way of speaking about the reading is to summarize, in order to identify that the reader has comprehended the story. If no other objective is met, this will be an excellent introduction, as the reader will think about a veteran's trauma and healing from PTSD. When a class discusses a simple review of the book, inevitably, each class participant will gain insight by listening to others' points of view.

Many readers are able to go beyond summarizing what they have read. The greatest benefits from reading, speaking, and writing come from examining the meaning of the book, not only as expressed by the author, but by relating the author's experience to their own experience.

Relating through writing and speaking results in greatly increased knowledge, and perhaps more importantly, in emotional learning as well. In some cases, members can pursue journaling as an added "homework assignment", allowing the time and privacy to reflect more deeply outside of the class setting.

The activities in this program are based on the revised version of *Bloom's Taxonomy* (a set of three hierarchal models used to classify educational learning objectives). The lessons outline various reading, speaking, and writing activities that promote deep learning. These activities require both thinking and feeling, and ultimately, can lead a class participant to take positive steps in his or her own life.

Lesson Objectives

Remember
- Recognize
- Recall

Understand
- Interpret
- Exemplify
- Classify
- Summarize
- Infer
- Compare
- Explain

Apply
- Execute
- Implement

Analyze
- Differentiate
- Organize
- Attribute

Evaluate
- Check
- Critique

Create
- Generate
- Plan
- Produce

How the Instructor Can Use This Book

Lesson Plans

The lessons follow the chronological narrative of the book. This is similar and familiar to veterans who have experienced trauma, the same way they tend to recall and tell their own stories. The exercises are separated into two categories: Section 1. Initial Symptoms of Acute Stress Disorder (ASD) and Initial Symptoms of Post Traumatic Stress Disorder (PTSD) and Section 2. Post War PTSD Symptoms and Resolution

The lessons are designed to help the class participant reconstruct his or her own experience, identify with the development of PTSD, and anticipate the gradual and cumulative nature of healing through both cognitive understanding and emotional growth.

Each exercise can be adapted to the timeframe of the group. Ideally, allow 45 minutes to one hour per lesson. Each is organized by:

Learning Objectives

Kissing the Tarmac offers many opportunities to remember, understand, apply, analyze, evaluate, and create. Each lesson may have one or more objectives. Some class members will need support with basic reading comprehension before they can consider the deeper meaning of the book and its application to their own lives.

Instruction

Always begin by confirming that class participants *remember* what they have read. Next, use class discussion to help the group to *understand* what they have read. After this review, the higher level objectives of the lesson will be attainable for all class members.

Response

Each lesson contains questions that prompt participants to explore at a higher level. Because some of these questions may be uncomfortable for participants, *instructors should never require participation or "grade" the responses to questions.* There truly is no right answer. Each participant will benefit from his or her own discoveries, while the instructor's role is to facilitate.

The instructor may wish to encourage the social processing of these questions through a spoken activity, such as individual sharing, pair sharing, or group sharing. Challenging and new ideas are better processed through *writing first*, with a discussion afterward. This allows the participant to think first, then to privately choose whether, and what, to share.

A Summary of
Kissing the Tarmac

Arriving in South Vietnam on the heels of the Tet Offensive in 1968, the author was assigned to Charlie Company, 2/501st Infantry, 101st Airborne Division operating in a region surrounding the ancient city of Hue. The unit suffered tremendous losses during his one-year tour of duty. Forty-nine members of his company were killed with three times as many wounded.

James was subjected to multiple traumatic events during eight consecutive months of combat before he was sent to a hospital in Da Nang with a severe leg infection.

Counseling was not offered to troops returning home in 1969, not even combat infantrymen. Soldiers were expected to assimilate back into civilized society and carry on with their lives—as if there were no lingering effects from the battlefield.

For many returning soldiers, like the author, that theory did not hold up. Symptoms manifested themselves as nightmares, anxiety, re-experiencing and avoidance. With the perception there was no place to turn to for relief, many sought out drugs and alcohol.

Time did mend the emotional wounds for many, but for some the reverse occurred. Older veterans who report a lifetime of only mild symptoms of PTSD, sometimes experience an increase later in life for a variety of reasons. Such was the case for the author who did not seek professional counseling until 2006.

Based on events recorded in his daily diary and 224 letters sent home during the war, James writes out his experiences as advised by his therapist. At first he finds it difficult, but over time the process becomes easier. After completing nine months of weekly therapy sessions, he realizes some relief from his symptoms and continues to write about his tour of duty for the next several years. He eventually uncovers the roots of his PTSD. With that knowledge in hand, he finds several effective methods to heal his emotional wounds that he shares with the reader.

Chapter Summary of Kissing the Tarmac

The Little Red Notebook- Introduction of the author's diary he kept during his tour of duty in Vietnam. It was used to record his thoughts, vent frustrations and allowed him to maintain some emotional balance.

The Letters
Overview of the 224 letters James wrote home. In 2006, he finally reads the letters (and his Notebook) and discovers traumatic experiences he put out of his mind for over four decades. The more he reads the more he realizes the letters contain the ingredients of his PTSD.

So This Is Combat
The author's first day in combat is almost his last. Their battalion chopper assault on a Vietcong encampment turns into a total disaster. He faces his first exposure to acute stress.

The Good Soldier
Highlights key events during eight months of combat where he is confronted with traumatic situations from the deaths of his buddies to torturing and killing enemy soldiers. He is plagued by endless skin infections and feelings of hopelessness. Periods of depression and anxiety develop from the constant trauma.

A Summary of *Kissing the Tarmac*

A Sense of Hope
While in the hospital for a month with a severe leg infection, the author gets back in touch with his true character and becomes more optimistic about surviving the war. He develops some inner strength resiliency for the first time.

The Way Home
A creative attempt to reach the Cam Ranh Bay airstrip following an airstrike that closes the Tan Son Nhut Air Base does not go as planned when his DC-3 nearly crashes.

The PTSD Years
Highlights events from 1970's-1990's where increasing PTSD symptoms affect his family and quality of life. The author experiences an emotional collapse at the Vietnam Memorial and seeks professional counseling.

Going Back, 2009
James returns to Vietnam with his wife on a ten-day tour of five cities from Ho Chi Minh City (Saigon) to Hanoi. In Hue, he confronts his "demons" by visiting key battlefields and conducts a memorial service for his forty-nine fallen buddies. It is his first major step towards catharsis healing.

Making Peace With It All
He visits the Vietnam Memorial for the third time in 2013 to make amends and move forward in his life.

What Worked For Me Might Work For You
The author shares ten emotional healing steps that have given him peace of mind.

HISTORICAL CONTEXT OF KISSING THE TARMAC

The first U.S. combat soldiers landed in Da Nang in 1965. When the last helicopter left Saigon in 1975, more than 58,200 troops had been killed with over 303,000 wounded, according to military sources. Enemy and civilian losses are estimated to have exceeded 1,000,000 lives.

James Hansen arrived in Vietnam at the end of the Tet Offensive in early 1968, when the North Vietnamese forces launched a nationwide attack on the Republic of South Vietnam. Intense fighting commenced, with over 1,000 U.S. soldiers dying weekly. His unit suffered their worst losses during this period.

That moment in history proved to be pivotal in America's support for the war as troop strength peaked at just over 500,000. While the antiwar movement had gained momentum and support starting in 1967 in the United States, it was the Tet Offensive that gave it a new purpose. Many Americans felt betrayed by the military and a government they believed had lied about the progress of the war effort.

The debate intensified from college campuses to the Congressional floor. The upcoming presidential election in November added more fuel to the fire. Both the Republican and Democratic Conventions became flashpoints for the debate that summer. War protests with graphic television coverage brought the drama into American homes each evening. Public opinion became increasingly negative.

Charlie Company was well aware of the growing dissention back home despite limited access to civilian news sources. Soldiers began having their doubts. Did America still support the war? Did our military leaders know what they were doing? Perhaps the most troubling question, was the war even *winnable*?

As the year went on, members of Charlie Company were increasingly confused as to their purpose in the war. Were they there to defeat the enemy, or just to maintain a presence? Often their missions just didn't make any sense.

This led to a growing opposition to the war among the ranks. In fact, several soldiers, including James, drew peace symbols on their helmets, signifying that while they were willing to serve their country, they were opposed to the war. Perhaps this message seems contradictory, but it was emblematic of the national mindset over America's role in Vietnam.

HISTORICAL EVENTS DURING THE TOUR OF DUTY

February, 1968
- President Johnson calls the Tet Offensive a complete failure. Tet is in fact a huge tactical victory for the United States, but it leads to a drastic decline in public support for the war.
- Walter Cronkite, the most influential new anchor of the time, tells Americans during his CBS Evening News broadcast that American leaders have been too optimistic and the Vietnam War will end in a stalemate.

March, 1968
- Approximately 300 Vietnamese civilians are slaughtered in the village of My Lai by U.S. troops led by Lieutenant William Calley. Initial reports state that sixty-nine Vietcong soldiers were killed and made no mention of civilians. The Army conceals the incident for a year.
- President Johnson tells the nation that he won't seek another term.

April, 1968
- James Earl Ray assassinates civil rights leader, Martin Luther King Jr., in Memphis.
- Secretary of Defense Clark Clifford announces that General Westmoreland's request for 206,000 additional soldiers will not be granted.
- Antiwar activists led by the Students for a Democratic Society (SDS) seize five buildings at Columbia University and hold school officials hostage.

May, 1968
- Peace talks begin in Paris but soon stall amid U.S. insistence that North Vietnamese troops withdraw from the south.
- The Vietcong launch a series of mortar and rocket attacks against 119 cities and military installations throughout South Vietnam.

June, 1968
- Senator Robert F. Kennedy is assassinated in Los Angeles just after winning the California Democratic Presidential Primary throwing the race into turmoil.

July, 1968
- Hanoi releases three U.S. prisoners of war in a move thought by many as a political attempt to affect public opinion in America.
- Congress passes a ten percent income tax surcharge to help defray the growing costs of the war.

August, 1968
- The Republican National Convention selects Richard Nixon as the Republican candidate. Mr. Nixon promises an honorable end to the war in Vietnam. The event is marred when 10,000 antiwar protesters are confronted by 26,000 police and National Guardsmen.

September, 1968
- The 900th U.S. Aircraft is shot down over North Vietnam.

October, 1968
- The United States releases fourteen North Vietnamese prisoners of war.
- President Johnson announces a complete cessation of the bombing of North Vietnam (Operation Rolling Thunder) in hopes of restarting the peace talks.

November, 1968
- Richard Nixon defeats Democrat Hubert Humphrey in the U.S. Presidential election.

December, 1968
- President-Elect Nixon appoints Henry Kissinger as his national security advisor.

January, 1969
- Peace talks begin in Paris between the American, South Vietnamese, North Vietnamese and Vietcong representatives.
- Richard Nixon is inaugurated as president.
- Melvin Laird becomes Secretary of Defense.

A Summary of *Kissing the Tarmac*

February, 1969
- The Vietcong attack 110 locations throughout South Vietnam, including Saigon.

March, 1969
- President Nixon authorizes Operation Menu, a secret campaign to bomb North Vietnamese supply bases located along the Cambodian border of Vietnam.

SECTION 1

Initial Symptoms of Acute Stress Disorder (ASD) and the Initial Symptoms of Post Traumatic Stress Disorder (PTSD)

Definitions

Post Traumatic Stress Disorder (PTSD)- The Veterans Administration's National Center For PTSD definition: "a mental health problem that some people develop after experiencing or witnessing a life-threatening event, like combat, a natural disaster, a car accident, or sexual assault. Symptoms include:

1. Reliving the event (also called re-experiencing symptoms)
2. Avoiding situations that remind you of the event
3. Negative changes in beliefs and feelings
4. Feeling keyed up (also called hyperarousal)"

Acute Stress Disorder (ASD)- The Veterans Administration's National Center's definition: "a psychiatric diagnosis...similar to PTSD, although the criteria for ASD contain a greater emphasis on dissociative symptoms and the diagnosis can only be given within the first month after a traumatic event. An ASD diagnosis requires that a person experience three symptoms of dissociation (e.g., numbing, reduced awareness, depersonalization, derealization or amnesia)."

Lesson 1

(after reading pp. 1-15)

Objectives
- To summarize the first traumatic events James experienced.
- To explain how these types of experiences can lead to the development of Acute Stress Disorder (ASD).

Instruction

1.) Consider each of the three examples of traumatic situations James experienced during his first day of combat. Describe each one in some detail.

　① Removing equipment from soldiers in body bags.

　② Witnessing soldiers being shot; one man died despite James's attempts to save his life.

　③ James walking "point." (The leading position with the highest risk of being wounded or killed).

2.) Identify what James's feelings were at each event. What words describe these feelings? List five emotional reactions he would have experienced.

3.) Read aloud the definition of ASD below.
Acute Stress Disorder (ASD)- "a psychiatric diagnosis…similar to PTSD, although the criteria for ASD contain a greater emphasis on dissociative symptoms and the diagnosis can only be given within the first month after a traumatic event. An ASD diagnosis requires that a person experience three symptoms of dissociation (e.g., numbing, reduced awareness, depersonalization, derealization or amnesia."

① Why would James be susceptible to ASD? Explain.

② Does James appear to suffer from these symptoms? Give examples from the story.

Response (*Advanced, optional*) How can you relate James's experience to your own life? Discuss or write a private journal entry to reflect upon your experience.

LESSON 2
(after reading pp. 27-28)

Objectives
- To understand how the act of killing enemy soldiers can generate conflicting emotions, creating ASD and early PTSD.
- To differentiate between the positive and negative emotions James experienced during and after killing others.

Instruction

1.) Review the three passages below. Discuss:
What emotions did James feel, in each of the three passages? How did James's thoughts and feelings change as he moved in time from the actual event to later, when he had the opportunity to recall and reflect?

> ① He looked in my direction just before the second grenade hit him in the waist. That moment was for every guy in Charlie Company who had gone home in a body bag. I was now a grunt to my very core—highly capable of hunting and killing the enemy, no matter how difficult the circumstances.
>
> Adrenaline surged through my body as I jumped to my feet. I was feeling much like I did when I shot my first deer as a teenager...My father couldn't have been prouder of me.

② The reality, that I had just done something that contradicted all of the psychological and social barriers against violence that I had learned growing up, began to sink in. All of the mind-altering training by the Army that told me it was "kill or be killed," and that it was "your patriotic duty to kill," had been called into question. My initial elation from getting my first enemy "kill" was replaced with numbness.

③ My mind reeled as I looked across the rice paddy at the two men lying dead next to the river. The responsibility for killing them was on my shoulders, and I would carry it for the rest of my life. Shit, I was now a professional killer.

2.) Consider the feeling James experienced. Are any of these feelings "right" or "wrong"? Why or why not? Discuss as a group.

Response (*Advanced, optional*) How can you relate James's experience to your own life? Discuss or write a private journal entry to reflect upon your experience.

Lesson 3

(after reading pp. 25-28)

Objectives
- To identify the coping methods James, and other ASD and PTSD victims often utilize.
- To attribute these coping behaviors to the cause/effect of trauma.
- To evaluate the effectiveness of these coping behaviors.

Instruction

1.) Review the three passages below. Discuss the coping methods James uses, such as avoiding, blocking, and repressing the memory of traumatic events.

① "Everything was going smoothly until one man in the first platoon tripped a 60-millimeter mortar booby trap. He was killed and another was badly wounded. Shortly after that, some of our own artillery rounds nearly hit us three times! All I could think of was what I did last Easter with you…
Love you and tons of affection, James"

② "We were hit by snipers and I got my first kill today—I caught two gooks in the open and got them with my 79. It was much like shooting deer (the same feeling) probably because I've developed so much hate for gooks killing my buddies."

③ "My hands began to tremble so badly that I couldn't hold the picture. It dropped on the ground face up. Scooping up a handful of mud laced with fresh blood, I covered the portrait in one motion. Using the sole of my combat boot, I methodically patted down the earth, in an attempt to forever bury the haunting image."

2.) Discuss:

① Why are these coping mechanisms useful?

② Was there anything else James could have done to protect himself from psychological trauma?

Response (*Advanced, optional*) How can you relate James's experience to your own life? Discuss or write a private journal entry to reflect upon your experience.

Lesson 4
(after reading pp. 36-40)

Objectives
- To identify how feelings and perceptions are affected by circumstances such as isolation and imminent danger.
- To explain how group dynamics contribute to abnormal conduct that an individual might not do alone.

Instruction

1.) Working with a partner or small group, review pages 36-40, "Pack Mentality."

List each word that describes the feelings and attitudes the soldiers are experiencing.

2.) Discuss:

① What are the causes of these feelings and perceptions?

② What "abnormal conduct" do the men engage in?

③ How does "peer pressure" play a role in their abnormal behavior?

④ How do their feelings and perceptions justify, in their minds at the time, their conduct?

⑤ Do we see some of these same feelings used to justify antisocial behavior and crimes in society today, outside of warfare?

Response (*Advanced, optional*) How can you relate James's experience to your own life? Discuss or write a private journal entry to reflect upon your experience.

Lesson 5
(after reading pp. 20-22)

Objectives
- To analyze the messages James wrote when under acute stress.
- To infer the way ASD and the development of PTSD effects communication with others.

Instruction

1.) Review and discuss the events of the story "The Erasing." (pg 20-21)

2.) Read the passages below. The journal entry was written on the same day as the events in "The Erasing," and the letter the day after.

> ① April 11, 1968
> On patrol today we killed two civilians kind of by accident. They ran and wouldn't stop so we opened up to see if they would stop. Some of the guys must have aimed a little low. Finally rained today— felt good.

> ② April 12, 1968
> Honey,
> Probably the most interesting thing that happened today was watching some ants moving a piece of my bread about a foot

or so in the last hour. I can't believe how strong they are. They just never give up.

I feel much better this morning than I did yesterday. It just wasn't a good day. I haven't felt so horrible in a long time. But today I am feeling better. I love you from the bottom of my heart and don't forget it. I prayed about 20 minutes straight last night and most of it was for you. I hope they are answered.

God Bless You, James

3.) Discuss:

① Is James "lying" to himself? Is he lying to his fiancée?

② Why did James choose to write these interpretations? Discuss each separately.

③ How did these versions serve him better than writing the actual events?

Response (*Advanced, optional*) How can you relate James's experience to your own life? Discuss or write a private journal entry to reflect upon your experience.

LESSON 6

(after reading pp. 36-41, 47-50, 53-55)

Objectives
- To interpret stories about other stressful aspects of military duty.
- To analyze how injustice, futility, and the lack of a clear purpose may contribute to ASD and early PTSD.

Instruction

1.) Read and discuss.
Unlike WWI, WWII and the Korean War, the conflicts in Vietnam, Iraq and Afghanistan had no front lines. In Vietnam, given geographic areas were occupied by American and South Vietnamese Army troops for hours, days or even weeks, but never with the intention of permanently holding that position. This strategy also did not create "safe zones" other than on individual bases. When soldiers were "outside the wire" (the perimeter of a base) they were subject to attacks from the enemy. Consequently, they could never let their defenses down, increasing their level of ASD and PTSD.

2.) Read and discuss.

① Divide into three groups, so each can review one of these three stories: "Pack Mentality" on pp. 36-41, "Be Done with Him" on pp.47-50, and "Inept and Stubborn" on pp.47-50.

② Each group will summarize for the class the injustices and incompetence that soldiers endure in each story.

③ Draw conclusions about how these circumstances may contribute to ASD and early PTSD.

Response (*Advanced, optional*) How can you relate James's experience to your own life? Discuss or write a private journal entry to reflect upon your experience.

LESSON 7
(after reading pp. 1-83)

Objectives
- To compare the coping methods James used during his tour of duty.
- To evaluate the effectiveness and benefits of various coping strategies.

Instruction
In addition to suppressing the memory of traumatic events, James took other actions as he tried to cope with the horrors of combat.

1.) Discuss both the pros and cons of each of these coping mechanisms.

① Using drugs and alcohol

② Keeping a daily journal and writing letters home

③ Reading magazines and newspapers from home

④ Listening to the Armed Forces Radio out of Da Nang

⑤ Talking with his buddies about troubling issues

⑥ Praying

2.) As a group, brainstorm a large list of coping mechanisms you have used to cope with stress. Write them so all can see and share the list.

3.) Discuss the uses and benefits, and any disadvantages, of the listed coping strategies.

Response (*Advanced, optional*) How can you relate James's experience to your own life? Discuss or write a private journal entry to reflect upon your experience.

LESSON 8
(after reading pp. 1-83)

Objectives
- To analyze the purpose and value of James's journal and letter writing.
- To understand the theory of cathartic writing in order to reduce anxiety.
- To produce a letter that processes stressful memories.

Instruction

1.) Review the letters that James wrote to his family and fiancée on pages 41, 45, 51, 56, 69, and 83.

2.) Discuss the purpose and value of these letters.

① Did the letters help James's family and fiancée? Did they cause conflict?

② What do you imagine James felt at the time he wrote them? Discuss for each letter.

3.) Read this passage aloud to the class:

> Mental health professionals agree that the act of handwriting what you are feeling following traumatic events offers positive benefits through cognitive processing. It allows cognitive processing as one purges. The brain releases the memory resulting in a reduction of anxiety for many individuals. The person will not necessarily forget the event going forward, but will often feel less anxious about it.

> ① Discuss the ideas of "cognitive processing" and "purging".

> ② "Writing soon after a traumatic event has occurred is beneficial. Even after time has passed, how can writing help with cognitive processing, purging, and relieving anxiety? Discuss.

4.) Write a letter to a loved one, past or present, about a stressful event in your life. You don't have to explain the event. You don't have to send the letter.

Response (*Advanced, optional*) How can you relate James's experience to your own life? Discuss or write a private journal entry to reflect upon your experience.

Lesson 9

(after reading pp. 71-73, 85-98)

Objectives
- To compare "engagement of the senses" with the numbness and dissociation that is often experienced in sustained periods of acute stress.
- To practice and apply "engagement of the senses."

Instruction

1.) Consider the two events when James got back in touch with his sensibilities (familiar and/or pleasurable tastes, smells, visual images, sounds, and touch feelings) following months of combat.
Review pages 71-73, when he was in the hospital, and 85-98, when he traveled to Sydney on his R & R

① List the five senses, and find specific examples of these familiar and pleasurable connections he made with his environment.

② Explain how each experience helped him refocus and reduce his acute stress.

2.) Make a list of the five senses. Under each, list three of your favorite sensory experiences: favorite foods, sights, etc. How many of these are readily available to you? How often do you seek them out?

3.) Take stock of your immediate sensory environment. Is there some sense pleasure you can seek out and use to enhance your reality? If necessary, look out a window at nature, massage aching muscles, or chew gum, etc. Focus on the pleasure, and notice the temporary alleviation of discomfort.

Response (*Advanced, optional*) How can you relate James's experience to your own life? Discuss or write a private journal entry to reflect upon your experience.

Lesson 10

(after reading pp. 1-117)

Objectives
- To recognize "hopefulness planning" and goal setting while undergoing extended acute stress.
- To practice and apply "hopefulness planning."

Instruction

1.) Consider the goals James sets for himself, particularly his goal of surviving the war.

- He repeatedly mentions his desire to make it through his tour of duty.
- He makes references to just surviving one day at a time.
- He keeps track of surviving each month on the opening page of his diary, including how many months he has left in Vietnam.
- He promises his family and fiancée that he will return to them, and that he will return a better man.

2.) Discuss:

① Is setting a goal of survival realistic, or even manageable, since he could not control the challenges he faced?

② Is there any reason *not* to set goals? Is there any reason *not* to hope for a good outcome?

③ Discuss how having his plans and goals could be beneficial in reducing ASD and early PTSD.

3.) Write a few "hopeful goals" for yourself. For the sake of the exercise, ignore the obstacles and focus on the feeling of hope. What do you deeply wish for? With consistent "hopefulness planning" could any of these "impossible dreams" come true? Why or why not?

If any of your goals are truly impossible, strike them from the list and add another "hopeful goal." Reinforce it daily.

Response (*Advanced, optional*) How can you relate James's experience to your own life? Discuss or write a private journal entry to reflect upon your experience.

Lesson 11

(after reading pp. 1-117)

Objectives
- To classify the kinds of traumatic events that can strengthen ASD and result in the development of PTSD symptoms
- To understand that PTSD symptoms persist once the actual stressor is removed.

Instruction

1.) In small groups or pairs, review the book to list five or more events that you felt were the most traumatic events that occurred during James's tour of duty.

   ① Although it may seem obvious, consider *why* these events were traumatic. In what way were they outside the scope of a 'normal' experience?

   ② What lasting impression would each leave with James? What intense feeling or sensory experience (the five senses) does he remember vividly?

   ③ In some cases, James was a witness to an event. In others, he was an active participant. How does being an active participant affect his feelings? Explain for each instance.

2.) James finishes his tour of duty and looks forward to going home.

① Can he forget these experiences? Should he try to forget?

② In a letter to his fiancée, James promises to return home "a better man." How can he become a better man, after all that he has experienced? Discuss.

Response (*Advanced, optional*) How can you relate James's experience to your own life? Discuss or write a private journal entry to reflect upon your experience.

SECTION 2

Post-War PTSD Symptoms and Resolution

LESSON 12

(after reading pp. 123-130)

Objectives
- To infer the effects of James's avoidance.
- To recognize how PTSD can affect the ability to respond effectively to challenges.

Instruction

1.) Discuss as a class: When people talked about the war, James would not participate in the conversation. He says, "I survived those times by remaining silent, burying my feelings deeper and deeper." When James revealed to friends or co-workers he was a Vietnam vet, they would sometimes say, "But *you* seem so normal." James says, "I struggled to respond." Why is it a struggle? Why does James stay silent?

2.) Review pages 123-130, and discuss.

① What evidence is there that James was "normal"? What did he do in the 1970s, '80s, and '90s to fit in to society?

② Was James successful and happy? Was his "normal" existence satisfying for him?

③ What would James's wife Karen have thought of him? Would she have thought he was "normal"?

④ James's son ran away from home after a confrontation about his addiction to drugs and alcohol. Under this stress, James's PTSD symptoms worsened. Did James respond effectively to this crisis? How could he have reacted differently?

3.) 3. One definition says "Avoidance refers to any action designed in preventing an uncomfortable emotion from occurring, such as fear, sadness or shame."

Write a private journal entry. Imagine that some well-meaning person said to you, "But *you* seem so normal." How would you answer them? Explore how you are "normal" and the ways your trauma has affected you. As you do, observe whether you struggle with avoidance. Do you experience uncomfortable emotions? What are they? Are you able to write an answer despite these feelings?

Response (*Advanced, optional*) How can you relate James's experience to your own life? Discuss or write a private journal entry to reflect upon your experience.

Lesson 13

(after reading pp. 123-130)

Objectives
- To identify PTSD symptoms
- To interpret PTSD triggers
- To attribute effects of PTSD to life choices and patterns

Instruction

1.) Review the passage on page 124, when James's dad was watching "Mission Impossible." What was James's reaction? Why? What behavior did James exhibit?

2.) Review pages 127-130. List the other PTSD symptoms James describes.

① Aside from isolated episodes, how was James's life, as a whole, affected by his PTSD during the thirty years after his return from the war? How might his life have been different if he had not suffered from PTSD?

② For each PTSD symptom, discuss whether there was a clear trigger. What symptoms did *not* have a trigger? Discuss as a group.

3.) In a private journaling activity, consider your own experience, post-trauma.

① Do you have symptoms of PTSD? What are they? Are there triggers that you can identify?

② Are there life choices and/or patterns that you see as outcomes of your PTSD? How might your life have been different? Are there patterns you would like to change?

4.) Some group members may choose to share these journal responses.

Response (*Advanced, optional*) How can you relate James's experience to your own life? Discuss or write a private journal entry to reflect upon your experience.

LESSON 14
(after reading pp. 127-138)

Objectives
- To understand the importance of sharing traumatic experiences
- To identify trustworthy friends/family members
- To plan future sharing

Instruction

1.) James did not share his combat experiences with his family or friends for decades. If he had discussed his experiences more openly, how might have it improved his relationships?

2.) Examine why and how to share traumatic stories.

① How can the act of talking about a traumatic event reduce the severity of PTSD symptoms? Discuss.

② Has sharing ever helped you? Give examples of conversations you've had about your trauma that helped you. Why did it help you?

3.) Sharing traumatic experiences with a mental health professional is considered very helpful, as they can maintain a level of objectivity and confidentiality. Discuss. Share a story of your positive experiences if you have worked with a professional and benefitted.

4.) Sharing traumatic experiences with trusted family members and friends is a healthy way to reduce stress and to develop healthy, deeper connections with others. Who are the people in your life capable of being supportive and non-judgmental?

List the people you can confidently share with. You may have already shared with them, or not.

5.) Even a trusted friend or relative may not be able to remain objective, or maintain confidentiality. Consider the people in your life who you find it difficult to confide in, and list them. Are there loved ones on this list? What obstacles prevent you from sharing with them? Can the obstacle be overcome? Would the relationship be improved?

6.) Choose one or more people from your lists. Circle the names of people you would like to share with to develop a deeper relationship.

Response (*Advanced, optional*) How can you relate James's experience to your own life? Discuss or write a private journal entry to reflect upon your experience.

Lesson 15

(after reading pp. 130-134)

Objectives
- To interpret the causes and effects of a flashback
- To recognize strategies to gain control during flashbacks

Instruction

1.) Ask a volunteer to read aloud "Here We Go Again" on pages 130-134. What are the triggers that cause James's flashbacks? As a group, make a list of them. Then discuss:

① How does James feel physically when the flashback occurs?

② Which senses does each of the triggers engage?

③ What emotion does James experience when each trigger is stimulated?

④ How do these triggers in the present correspond to the past?

2.) Consider the context and circumstances. What kind of day was James having? Given his environment, how was he more vulnerable to experiencing a flashback? Discuss.

3.) Some of James's reactions are very strong. What does he feel toward the man with the stick? Why? Is the emotion affected by the flashback, or is it an appropriate reaction to the present situation?

4.) James makes several attempts to regain his control. What actions does he take to counter the flashback and the anxiety he experiences? How do his actions help? Are these good techniques to use?

5.) What techniques can help with flashbacks? As a group, brainstorm a list and discuss. Consider things you can do to address flashbacks:

- Physical response
- Emotional response
- Actions you can take
- "Self talk" (things you might say to yourself)

Response (*Advanced, optional*) How can you relate James's experience to your own life? Discuss or write a private journal entry to reflect upon your experience.

Lesson 16

(after reading pp. 134-136)

Objectives
- to recognize an emotional breakdown
- to identify and differentiate purging and reprocessing memories
- to understand the potential benefits of recovering repressed memories

Instruction

1.) Read this passage, James's "emotional meltdown," as he described it, at the Vietnam Memorial in 2004.

> ...emotions buried for decades erupted with volcanic force, followed by an unthinkable confession.
> "I fucking killed her. I shot a twelve-year old girl when she wouldn't stop running away," I heard myself say again and again.
> On one level I knew they were my words, but on another, I had no conscious knowledge of this tragic event. What girl? I never shot a child. This did not happen. Wouldn't I have remembered such a horrid event?

Discuss.

Winning the War with PTSD

① Do we remember everything we experience?

② Why do we sometimes repress memories?

2.) On page 135, James describes how his mind gradually processed the repressed memory. "…the reality of what happened thirty-six years earlier began to materialize…as if I was viewing it from a distant perch through a camera's telescopic lens." Read aloud the rest of the passage.

① How does this imaginary camera protect James's emotions as he recovers his memory?

② How does the camera help him to "arrive" at the memory he has repressed?

③ What does he see that confirms to him this is a real memory?

3.) Is James's "emotional meltdown" painful? Was "purging" the memory a horrible experience? Review the passage, and discuss.

4.) Is there a benefit to getting a painful memory back? Do memories help healing? How can this help to relieve PTSD? Discuss.

Response (*Advanced, optional*) How can you relate James's experience to your own life? Discuss or write a private journal entry to reflect upon your experience.

Lesson 17

(after reading pp. 137-138)

Objectives
- To summarize the benefits of writing about traumatic experiences as part of PTSD therapy.
- To generate a plan for journal writing topics

Instruction

1.) James's therapist asked him to write out key war-related experiences. Like many PTSD sufferers, he found this practice exceptionally healing. James began by reviewing things that had already been written – his notebook. He used the notebook and his letters as "prompts," as they gave him topics to write about and to get started.

2.) Do you prefer to have a prompt that gives you a clear writing topic? Or do you prefer to explore your experiences by "free writing" without topics or questions? What are the pros and cons? Discuss.

3.) James's therapist said, "The more you write about things that haunt you, the better you will feel. A good starting point might be your first day in combat. I imagine that will be tough. If that's too difficult, you can always begin with lighter topics and work your way into the more challenging situations. Trust me, it will work."

① How would it feel to write about a lighter topic, rather than a difficult one? What would be the rewards? Discuss.

② How would it feel to *complete* writing about a more painful traumatic experience? What would be the obstacles you would have overcome? What would be the rewards? Discuss.

4.) If you were going to write a journal, how would you approach the assignment the therapist gave to James? Would you begin at the beginning and go forward chronologically? Or would you pick easier topics and work up to the harder ones? Or another method? Discuss.

5.) Make a private list of topics you would write about. Refer to each traumatic experience with just a word or phrase- you'll know what you meant. After you have generated up to 10 topics, stop and review them. Place an L next to the "lighter" topics you could tackle more easily, and write a D next to topics that would be more difficult and painful to explore. Keep this list to inspire you to write. It can be your prompt.

Response (*Advanced, optional*) How can you relate James's experience to your own life? Discuss or write a private journal entry to reflect upon your experience.

Lesson 18

(after reading pp. 139-151)

Objectives
- To interpret *re-experiencing* traumatic events as a therapeutic exercise.
- To critique the method and pace of re-experiencing trauma.

Instruction

1.) James traveled back to Vietnam on the fortieth anniversary of his return from the war. Why would he want to do this? Why not? Discuss.

2.) Review pp. 139-151, and discuss:

① How had Vietnam changed? In what ways was it different from when James served his tour of duty there?

② How did the people of Vietnam behave and how did they react to James? Did they consider him an enemy?

③ The old battlefields were gone. What happened to them? How did James react?

④ Why is it particularly significant that the Citadel, which was "ground zero" during the Tet Offensive, was still standing, mostly undamaged?

3.) Read aloud pp. 140-142, "War Remnants Museum."

① List the triggers James experiences at the museum.

② For each trigger, he reflects back on the war. What painful thoughts do these exhibits prompt, in addition to the specific wartime memories they evoke?

4.) James visited the War Remnants Museum on his first day in the country.

① How could he have planned his timing better?

② How could he have arranged for more emotional support?

③ How could he have handled this part of his re-experiencing journey better?

④ What conclusion did James draw after he left the museum? Did he achieve a healthy acceptance, despite his suffering? Discuss.

Response (*Advanced, optional*) How can you relate James's experience to your own life? Discuss or write a private journal entry to reflect upon your experience.

LESSON 19

(after reading pp. 144-151)

Objectives
- To interpret *re-experiencing* traumatic events as a therapeutic exercise.
- To seek new information in order to supplement the past with a new experience.

Instruction

1.) Read aloud from pp 144-145, beginning on the fourth paragraph that begins, *Reaching the bridge where the highway crossed the Song Bo...*

① James looks around to see the mountains, now green. How does he feel?

② James remembers the deaths he witnessed, and concludes "I sensed I would never be able to shake my deep resentment toward everything about this war." Is that feeling an indication of PTSD, or is it a reasonable feeling? He says "They gave everything... and we still lost the war," I replied. "It is just a fucking shame." Is that attitude a result of PTSD, or is it psychologically healthy?

43

③ James dropped roses from the bridge into Song Bo River. What might the roses represent? Do they have more than one meaning for James?

④ Clearly, James had planned this ceremony in advance. What do you think he hoped it would accomplish? How could this gesture help to heal PTSD?

⑤ James's wife took a photo of him at the bridge that is similar to one taken during the war. How can having these two photographs help James to heal?

2.) James wrote, "My intent was to…return to the source of my war memories and replace them with contemporary images of this rapidly progressing Third World country."

For James, there were specific places in Vietnam that had haunted him. He sought out these places to gain closure. Is it always a *place* that must be revisited? Must we visit there, literally? How else can we visit the past for closure? Would using the internet for a virtual visit serve the same purpose? Discuss other ways to re-experience the past in order to create new, positive memories.

Response (*Advanced, optional*) How can you relate James's experience to your own life? Discuss or write a private journal entry to reflect upon your experience.

Lesson 20
(after reading PP 1-156)

Objectives
- To summarize the treatment of PTSD in military veterans
- To plan for the best healing experience

Instruction

1.) PTSD wasn't documented accurately until the mid-1980s. The military in the Vietnam War era did not realize the importance of screening for veterans that were suffering from war stress. What impact did this have on soldiers like James, who only learned of PTSD after suffering its symptoms, undiagnosed, for many years? Discuss.

2.) Are you familiar with how the military screens veterans returning from war zones today? Do they effectively route these veterans toward appropriate help? Share your knowledge with the group. Do you think the military's methods are effective?

3.) Today they do screen for PTSD, but if a returning soldier completes a form with certain boxes checked, he/she may be subject to additional testing and delays in going home. Young soldiers say they often lie about their actual condition because they just want to be released as quickly as possible. Should the military require mandatory screening for everyone as part of the DEROS process?

4.) What could the military do to ease the difficult transition of soldiers returning to civilian life? As a group, make a list of the processes and resources that the military and our civilian society does provide. Make a list of services it should provide, but does not currently offer. Discuss.

5.) Write a list of the services and support you have utilized so far in your healing of PTSD. Assess:

① Has it been "enough" or do you continue on the journey to heal?

② Refer to the lists created by the group in exercise 4. Which of these resources might help you with your PTSD?

③ Make a list of what you intend to do to proactively heal in the future.

Response (*Advanced, optional*) How can you relate James's experience to your own life? Discuss or write a private journal entry to reflect upon your experience.

Lesson 21

(after reading pp. 153-156)

Objectives
- To explain how premeditated actions can provide closure.
- To create a letter that can provide closure.

Instruction

1.) Review pages 153-156. James calls this section "Making Peace with it All." Exactly what does James do to "make peace," and is he successful?

2.) Have a volunteer read this passage aloud:

> "Guys, I am here to honor each one of you and make peace with the past," I said, in a soft voice. "I deeply respect all of you for giving your lives for our country. To think that over 58,000 Americans died in the end… and, other than this humble monument, we have little to show for it. For the last forty years, I hated our nation's leaders for allowing this to happen."
>
> Continuing on, I said, "This affected every aspect of my life… from my marriage, to the way I raised my sons, to what I have accomplished over the years. And all the way the peace of mind I was seeking was never within reach.

When I returned home after my last visit here in 2004, I began seeing a therapist. He got me to realize that I had to let my resentment go. I now understand I shouldn't feel guilty for serving in the war and surviving while you did not. I had only done what my country had asked me to do. I needed to refocus my feelings. It has been a long process but I am ever closer to my goal."

"I wouldn't be alive today had it not been for all of you covering my back," I said. "Thank you all from the bottom of my heart for your dedication and conviction to the men of Charlie Company, 2/501st Infantry, 101st Airborne. God bless you."

3.) Write your own letter to your brothers–in-arms or to those who have been tragically lost in your life.

- What do you wish you could say to them about the experiences you shared?
- How have they mattered to you?
- What can you say to them about the person you have become?
- James ends his letter with gratitude. Is there something that you can be grateful for? If so, give thanks.

Response (*Advanced, optional*) How can you relate James's experience to your own life? Discuss or write a private journal entry to reflect upon your experience.

Lesson 22

(after reading pp 157-162)

Objectives
- To analyze which of James's actions and recommendations could help you address your PTSD symptoms.
- To generate a list of other, additional actions that you believe you need to heal.

Instruction

1.) Review the ten action steps the author took to overcome his PTSD. Discuss the merits of each one.

① Find your "Mother Ocean"

② Reach out to family and friends for support

③ Embrace your veteran status

④ Write down what haunts you (and burn it in your fireplace)

⑤ Seek out a qualified therapist and/or veteran support group

⑥ Challenge your sense of helplessness by assisting veterans and others who are in need

⑦ Address negative behavior that interferes with healing

⑧ Reconnect with your faith

⑨ Find a way to celebrate being alive every day

⑩ Go back to your "battlefield"

2.) Place a checkmark next to the number of the list above if you feel you have already fully explored that path toward healing.

3.) Circle the number of any of the listed actions that seem appropriate for you to do. Reflect on why it would help. Take a moment to visualize how you would proceed to take this step.

4.) Consider other actions you hope to take. Write them out to add them to your list of goals.

5.) As a group, share your plans for action in the future.

Response (*Advanced, optional*) How can you relate James's experience to your own life? Discuss or write a private journal entry to reflect upon your experience.

Lesson 23

Objectives
- To recognize PTSD healing
- To create positive milestones in PTSD recovery

Instruction

1.) James said, "I needed to refocus my feelings. It has been a long process but I am ever closer to my goal." He acknowledges that healing from PTSD is a process, rather than a disorder that is on/off. Did James heal in clear stages? Did he know at each point that he was making progress? Discuss.

2.) When the story end, do you think James is fully healed, and will never experience a PTSD symptom again? Will it continue to impact his work and relationships? Discuss.

3.) James and his wife have several meaningful celebrations to mark the occasion of his healing and closure. Discuss:

① James said, "My only experience with the holiday period previously was the horrific Tet Offensive of 1968." Now he and his wife celebrate Tet together. "Tet is the traditional Vietnamese New Year…This is the time to forgive and forget, and to pay off debts." How is their celebration of Tet a powerful milestone for James?

② James's wife captured the moment in a photograph when James visited the Song Bo Bridge. This photograph is very precious to him. Why?

③ James's wife also took a photo of them together, drinking a champagne toast in Vietnam. How is she helping him to heal? How does her involvement affect their marriage?

4.) In a private journal entry, retrace your journey with PTSD. Have you had any healing milestones, perhaps ones that you did not appreciate at the time? List any of your successes. (Refer to Lesson 22 for a reminder.)

5.) Join a small group. Taking turns, share each success story. Give each person applause and affirmation. Each group can share a few special milestones with the whole class.

6.) Set a goal. In the future, every milestone and every small victory in your healing should be celebrated. Think of who to share your story with, how to tell them of your success, and how to celebrate and remember the moment. Take a picture.

Resources

PTSD Specific Support
The National Center for Post Traumatic Stress Disorder
www.ptsd.va.gov
Also: www.afterdeployment.org

Find a Therapist Trained In PTSD
http://ptsd.about.com/od/ptsdbasics/tp/txproviders.htm

References and Helpful Books

- *Haunted by Combat*, 2007, Praeger Security International, Daryl S. Paulson and Stanley Krippner
  Understanding PTSD in war veterans.

- *A Temporary Sort of Peace: A Memoir of Vietnam*, 2007, Indiana Historical Society Press, Jim McGarrah
  A Vietnam veteran works to overcome bouts with PTSD.

- *The Timeline of the Vietnam War*, 2008, Thunder Bay Press, Kevin Daugherty and Jason Stewart
  A comprehensive timeline of the Vietnam War.

- *Soft Spots*, 2009, St. Martin's Press, Clint Van Winkle
  A veteran of the war in Iraq struggles with PTSD upon his return home and discusses an institutional treatment program.

- *Overcoming Trauma and PTSD,* 2012, New Harbinger Publications, Inc., Sheela Raja, PhD
  A self-help workbook.

- *The PTSD Workbook, Third Edition,* 2016, New Harbinger Publications, Inc., Mary Beth Williams, PhD, LCSW, CTS, Soili Poijula, PhD
  A self-help workbook.

Acknowledgements

The author would like to extend his deep appreciation to the following individuals for their contributions to this publication:

Todd Adamson, Psy.D., Clinical Director, "Outside The Wire," U.S. VETS Initiative, Los Angeles, CA.

Susan Michael, Psy.D., Clinical Director, U.S. VETS Initiative, Long Beach, CA.

www.ingramcontent.com/pod-product-compliance
Lightning Source LLC
Chambersburg PA
CBHW072106290426
44110CB00014B/1846